Thirteen at Last!

Elizabeth Rosales-Alcantara

Copyright© 2024 by Elizabeth Rosales-Alcantara
All rights reserved. This book or any portion thereof may not be reproduced or used in any manner whatsoever without the express written permission of the publisher except for the use of brief quotations in a book review.

Limits of Liability and Disclaimer of Warranty

The author and publisher shall not be liable for your misuse of this material. This book is strictly for informational purposes. The purpose of this book is to educate. The author and publisher do not guarantee anyone following these techniques, suggestions, tips, ideas, or strategies will become successful. The author and publisher shall have neither liability nor responsibility to anyone with respect to any loss or damage caused, or alleged to be caused, directly or indirectly by the information contained in this book. Views expressed in this publication do not necessarily reflect the views of the publisher.

Printed in the United States of America
Young Authors Initiative; Keen Vision Publishing, LLC
www.publishwithkvp.com
ISBN: 979-8-325356-65-0

For teenagers going through the challenges of life's unexpected changes.

CONTENTS

Chapter One
A Morning Full of Nightmare   7
Chapter Two
There's Always Cats and Music   13
Chapter Three
Icecream with Friends   17
Chapter Four
Twelve Weeks   19
Chapter Five
Concerning   21
Chapter Six
Goodbye   23
Connect with the Author   26

Chapter One

A MORNING FULL OF NIGHTMARES

August 5th was the day I turned thirteen. The day everything changed. It was a warm summer morning here in New York. The year was 2023, and I was headed into my first day of 8th grade. *Ugh, I have math first period this year AGAIN.* I said in my head as I looked at my schedule. I could feel a knot in my stomach forming as I imagined the math equations this year. Math was never my best subject. My twin brother Leo was sitting next to me, eating cereal. He realized the visibly upset expression on my face.

"What the heck, Aria! Your face is as pale as a ghost! You're seriously freaking me out." He said as he stared me up and down with a disgusted look.

"Haha, very funny. I got math first period again this year. I absolutely HATE math." I said in response to his comment.

"So, why don't you just quit school?" That's my twin

brother.

"You're so dumb sometimes, Leo." The time was now 7:30. "C'mon, Leo. We have to go now."

"Yeah, yeah, whatever."

"Bye, ma!" We both yell out to Mom, who is in the kitchen.

"Bye, kids!" she yelled in response. It's a ten-minute walk from home to school, so we arrived around 7:40. On our way to homeroom, we parted ways, and I met up with Naomi and Kali.

"Hey guys."

"He- whoa," Kali says.

"Erm, why is your face all pale-ish??"

"Math class first period again," I replied.

Naomi jumped in, "Dang that must suck." Naomi and Kali both looked really alike. They both had long brown cappuccino-colored hair with dark brown eyes. However, their styles were really different.

"Dude, I—..."

"...WHAT?" Someone yells from a distance. We continued to hear yelling and eventually checked it out. Apparently, some kid was REALLY upset at their schedule. *But what can you do?* The homeroom teacher really didn't care, and it showed 'cause all she did was tell the kid to sit down in an unbothered tone. I guess that was a good thing. She was a rather young teacher, so it makes sense why she was way more laid back compared to the other teachers.

The bell rang a couple of minutes later. Everyone scrambled around the halls, trying to find their classes. Once the tardy bell rang, I was already in math class.

"Everyone, take a seat!" The teacher introduced himself as Mr. Davidson. As much as I didn't like math, Mr. D. seemed like a pretty chill guy. Also, since it was the first day of school, we didn't do much other than go over class procedures and rules we were expected to follow. These are basic things every teacher explains. No food, no phones, no fighting, blah blah blah. I'm a pretty good student, if I do say so myself. I end up not even paying attention. That was until Mr. D. brought up what we'd be learning this year. Algebra, Data Analysis, Geometry, even hearing the word "math" made me feel sick inside. What's worse is that this class is an hour long. Sitting in this class made me think about how different 8th grade really was.

It made me miss 6th grade, but not really. 6th grade was horrible. Sure, it was an easy year academically. But, outside of classes, it was a whole different story. It wasn't fun having fake friends, being left out all the time, and knowing you were talked about. Nothing about 6th grade was fun. The only thing I remember of that year was being miserable. Multiple unsettling thoughts. To my "friends," I was nothing.

For a while, I actually believed everyone thought this about me, too. Being constantly ignored and being made fun of was really getting to me. It started affecting my home life and grades. I became a different person, according to my mother, whom I cried to. Moving to New York was the best decision we made in our lives. Here, life is nicer. Here, I have real friends. I thought about this for the whole class. I snapped out of my train of thought when the loud bell

THIRTEEN @ LAST!

rang. Second period!! I was relieved. I had second-period band, so this was good for me. The band was one thing I was passionate about. Having been playing my trombone since I was 11, I was already good. However, there was just one problem. I hadn't practiced all summer.

Playing for the first time in months frustrated me. However, it was comforting to see that my section was struggling, too, and it wasn't just me. I also took this class with Benny. Benny was across the class in the woodwinds section with his flute. Benny was one of the taller guys in our grade. He had fluffy, short black hair and brown eyes. His style consisted of baggy street clothing. Benny had told me he was struggling as well. Most of us were, to be fair. This stressed Mr. Brown, our band director.

We were a really small band compared to the other bands in our county. This didn't bother us since we sounded better than most of those bands. At the end of class, we put everything back, and Benny and I made small talk. It could have been a longer conversation if the bell hadn't rung. At least 3rd period was a class I had with all my friends. P.E. was a class where we got to just chill. Although I had a low grade in physical education, I never tried to bring that up. My friends and I just sat back and talked about the latest news in this class. Sometimes, we participated, but most of the time, we didn't.

"Have you guys gone to English class yet?" Estrella asked. Estrella had shoulder-length black hair with blonde highlights. Her style was pretty basic. T-shirts and jeans were her go-to.

A MORNING FULL OF NIGHTMARES

"No, what about you guys?" Kali answered.

"Yeah, I have. The teacher is pretty cool." Naomi mentioned.

"I have English next with my brother, Leo," I announced.

Leo was similar to Benny, perhaps that's why Benny and I became friends. Leo was energetic and loud, often perceived as the "class clown." We were twins, but we were very different.

Once fourth period rolled around, it was lunchtime. Lunch at my school wasn't the best, but not the worst. Spaghetti was not the best. Luckily for me, we had hotdogs. You really can't mess up hotdogs. The lunch period was the best period. We got to mess around and enjoy lunch.

Bummer! The lunch bell rang, and we headed back to the fourth period. All my classes from the fourth period were pretty much talking about the same thing. By the seventh period, I was already feeling sleepy. As I was about to doze off, the last bell rang.

The bell! I yell out in my head. *Time to go home.* I made my way to Mom's car. Waiting for Leo, Mom asked about my day.

"It was kind of boring. All we did was talk about rules." I informed her. After what seemed like forever, Leo got in the car, and we drove off.

Chapter Two

THERE'S ALWAYS CATS AND MUSIC

Mom pulled the car up to the driveway, and we got off. As she unlocked the door, my cat, Luna, made a sudden appearance.

"Hey, Luna!" I said. In response, she rubbed on my blue jeans. I let Luna in and put away my stuff. I pulled out my phone to see what was happening in the group chat. My phone had been blowing up since school ended. I scrolled through the past texts and read them silently to myself.

"Hey, does anyone want to go out and get ice cream in a couple?" Estrella asked.

By the looks of it, everyone agreed to go. Naturally, I texted back with a reply. "Let me ask my mom."

I yelled out to my mom, who was in the other room, "Mom, can I go out with friends in a couple?"

"Sure, Ari! Just don't stay out too late!"

"Thanks, Mom!" I yelled out in response. I returned to

THIRTEEN @ LAST!

the group chat and texted, "My mom said yes!"

"Alright, so everyone's down?"

Yep's and yea's filled the chat.

"Let's go at 6," Benny responded. I can tell he was excited cause' it only took him about five seconds to type that out. Everyone agreed. I looked down at my phone for the time.

Hmm, it's 5:04. I calculated the time in my head. *If I finish getting ready at 5:20, I have time to eat dinner. I'm a fast eater most of the time, so that would only take 10 to 20 minutes. Perfect.* I put my phone on the charger and headed to my room. While getting ready, my phone made a slight sound—ping! I looked on the group chat to see an image of a cat holding a lollipop attached to a message, "See you guys there!"

After ten minutes or so, I made my way to the kitchen. I got a plate and ate dinner. My twin brother, Leo, walked in. "Why does it look like you're gonna head out? What did I miss? Also, why do we wear the same type of clothes? Oh man, now we REALLY look like twins." He blurted out altogether.

"WOAH. Can you repeat that? I didn't get ANY of that. Also, you didn't miss anything; I'm just going out with friends. And, what's wrong with looking like twins when we literally ARE twins." I asked.

There was silence for a second. This was probably the most random conversation I've had with my brother, considering the fact he always talked about random stuff. Leo and I talked a bit about school and whatnot for a little while. I turned on my phone screen. It was 5:36.

I have to get going. The place is pretty far when you're walking. I said to myself as I searched around the house for Mom. *Weird. She's usually in the kitchen or living room.* The only place I had not checked was my parent's own room. I made my way to their door. I pressed my cheek against the door, hoping to hear my mom or dad. I listened for a good amount of time and heard mumbling. It sounded like my mom and dad were discussing about something. I couldn't make out what they were saying, but I could tell it wasn't good due to the reactions I got from them once they spotted me. They looked at me with a sort of disappointed face for a split second. After about five seconds, my mother stood up and walked towards me.

I explained how I needed to get going if I was going to hang out with friends. "I won't be back too late!" I promised. Although I was suspicious of what my parents were up to, I brushed it off and didn't think too much of it.

We live in a pretty average-sized town, so there were a few stray cats I would feed every day. "Hey guys, did ya miss me?" I talked to the cats as if they could understand me. I wished cats could talk. I watched the cats finish the bowl of food and water I had put out for them. I needed to get going, or I would be late! "Bye, Gatitos!" Gatitios means kitties in Spanish. I mixed Spanish with English any chance I got.

I listened to music the rest of the way. I liked a wide variety of music genres. Music had always made me happy. When I listened to music, it was like time slowed down, and I was the only one who existed. People usually thought I was sad all the time, but I just listened to music.

Chapter Three

ICECREAM WITH FRIENDS

I finally made it to the ice cream place. I looked at the phone once more. 5:56. *I'm right on time.* I thought to myself. I checked the group chat and saw that almost everyone had arrived. I scrolled on my phone to pass the time when I suddenly got a notification from the band group chat.

"Practice tomorrow!! (ENDS AT 4:00!!)"

Great! I loved the band so much, so that was exciting for me! By the time I put my phone away, Estrella was already next to me. I jumped into realization. "You scared me! How were you so quiet? How long have you been standing there?!"

"Relax, Aria! I've only been here for two minutes. Also, I'm not sure how I was so quiet." As Estrella answered all my questions, suddenly, everyone poured in. We ordered our ice cream. I got vanilla with chocolate syrup and sprinkles! We made our way out once everyone ordered and headed to a nearby park. By the time we got there, the sun was setting. It was a beautiful sight to be there and experience. You'd better believe I took a lot of pictures! Afterwards, we laughed and ran around. It was about 8:20 when Benny and I decided to leave because we had band practice the next day. We lived in different neighborhoods, so we said our goodbyes to everyone and went our separate ways.

Once I got home, I took a shower and checked my phone. I posted the pictures and tagged my friends. Everyone seemed happy and pleased with the post. By then, the time was 10:30. I brushed my teeth and hopped into bed. That night, I had a dream. More so a nightmare.

It was sixth-grade year, and I was in the center of a circle formed by a group of people. Their faces were blurred, so I couldn't tell who was there. I knew it was sixth grade because I saw the outside of my old middle school. They were saying something, but I couldn't make out what was being said. It was kinda like the feeling I got when my parents were mumbling. I suddenly woke up, sweating. I processed what just happened. I assured myself over and over that it was only a dream. I got up to get a glass of water. What a weird dream.

Chapter Four

TWELVE WEEKS

After school, I texted my mom to tell her about band practice. After confirming with my mom, I headed to the band room and got my trombone. This was the happiest I had been since school started. Playing trombone was where most of my happiness came from. It made me happy because ever since I started playing, I felt like I could put all my energy into it, and it made a better sound.

Seeing music notes was a familiar feeling. I had definitely grown in my skills. Since I was eleven, I've learned how to play complex pieces. However, I hadn't played in twelve weeks, so I had a lot of work to do. After the warmups, I already felt more confident in my playing. We didn't have any projects to work on since school had just started. Although I was enjoying myself, I could tell the other trombonists weren't.

"I'm not sure how you can enjoy this so much. Sure, I

love band, but I don't think I could be passionate about it and do it forever like how you plan on doing it," a band mate said.

"I guess I do like it a lot," I replied.

"I think that's good. You found something you like, and you're passionate about it!" He said with a smile.

"Alright, guys, I think that's it for today! You may put up and be dismissed! Have a good rest of your day, guys!" Mr. Brown said.

I put away my music and trombone and head out. I walked out of the school and made my way home. I listened to music the whole way. It was one of the best feelings I had felt. Life was finally going smoothly. I had good grades, I had cool friends, and I was playing the trombone again. Being thirteen was better than any other age. When I was 8, I broke my arm after playing on the playground. When I was ten, I lost a district spelling bee in the first round. The list goes on and on. Thirteen was already off to a better start than any other year. I knew it would be the best year yet!

Chapter Five

CONCERNING

While walking home, I got an unexpected call from Leo. "What's up?" I answered.

"Hey, Aria, Dad says you need to come home and hurry." He said with panic in his voice.

"Uhh, sure," I responded and hung up. Concern grew on me as I started wondering what could have possibly happened. It was strange for my dad to act like that. He usually had a fun personality and wouldn't rush me to come home. I tried to get home as fast as I could. Whenever I got home, my mom was always making dinner, and today wasn't any different. My dad wasn't even home yet, so I was confused about why I needed to come home. At first, I thought Leo was messing with me.

"Leo, why'd you lie to me?!" I said when I saw him.

Leo snapped back, "I didn't lie to you! Dad called me and told me to tell you to come home on time so we could eat together. Apparently, he and Mom have something to talk about with us at dinner. I don't think it's good based on Dad's tone when he told me to call you."

"What could it be? Do you have any idea?" I asked.

"No, not really. Though, I have been noticing that lately, Mom and Dad have been talking less." Leo suggested.

"Really? I noticed that they've been mumbling lately." I shared.

"Who knows? Guess we'll have to wait till dinner!" Leo shrugged.

"Yeah, I guess so," I said.

Dinner came around, and Leo and I were feeling worried. At the dinner table, it was awfully quiet. Leo and I exchanged looks. A couple of minutes passed by until Mom spoke up. "Aria, Leo. Your father and I have something to tell you!"

By the tone of it, I couldn't quite put my finger on what she meant. I looked over at Leo to see he was confused as well. "Kids, don't freak out when we say this, but—" Mom began.

Leo and I looked at each other with worried faces. Mom continued, "Your father and I are getting a divorce."

Suddenly, it seemed like everything got quiet, and time slowed down.

Chapter Six

GOODBYE

At that moment, I did not know what to think. *What's gonna happen to me and Leo?* Before I could say anything, Leo was already asking questions.

"Calm down," Dad reassured him. Although it was never clear why they divorced, they did. Dad would stay in New York, and Mom would move to Mexico. It was already decided that Leo and I would stay with Mom and visit Dad on holidays.

"When are we leaving, mom?" I asked.

"Probably next week." She responded.

In the back of my mind, I'm thinking, *Why so soon?* After dinner, I texted the group chat. "Guys, we need to meet up at the same park from the other day in the next hour!" Luckily, everyone responded quickly with agreement. I ran the whole way to save time, and to my surprise, everyone was already there.

THIRTEEN @ LAST!

"What happened, Aria?" Naomi asked.

"My parents are getting divorced, and Leo and I have to live in Mexico with our mom! I know it's sudden; I just found out myself like an hour ago." I blurt out quickly.

Suddenly, it went silent, mostly because everyone was trying to process what I had just said. Kali was the first to understand; she was the smartest.

"So, you're leaving? Forever?" Kali asked sadly. At this point, everyone was caught up and staring at me, waiting for a response.

"Yeah, but I'll be back for holidays," I told them.

"When are you leaving?" Benny and Estrella synchronized.

"Next week." I immediately responded.

"Why so soon??!!" Everyone wondered out loud.

"I don't know. I don't know why they didn't tell me sooner." I replied sadly.

"Aria, it's Friday. If you're going to pack and prepare for your trip, it'll take up the whole week! We won't see you at all anymore! Is this our last time seeing you in person?" Benny asked.

"I guess so…" I look down to avoid eye contact with everyone.

"Let's take a group photo on my Polaroid; I have it with me right now," Benny said. "One…Two…THREE! Click!" Benny handed it to me with a slight smile. "For the memories!"

"Thanks. Well, it's getting late; I better get going." I told everyone

"Yeah."

GOODBYE!

We hugged and said our goodbyes. When I got home, I was devastated. *But what could I do?* I thought thirteen would be my year. I guess not.

Mexico is okay, but New York will always be home.

CONNECT WITH THE AUTHOR

The Young Authors Initiative (YAI) is a Keen Vision Publishing (KVP) program designed to help young writers, especially those in middle school, achieve their goal of becoming published authors.

ELIZABETH ROSALES-ALCANTARA is a 2024 YAI writer. She enjoys writing as a hobby. In her spare time, she loves doing anything related to music. She hopes to one day become very successful and have a stable life and family.

For more information about ELIZABETH or YAI, visit www.publishwithkvp.com

Made in the USA
Columbia, SC
01 February 2025